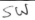

SW

Casting Off the Corsets

A Brief History of Underwear

By Dul

First published 2011
© Dulcie Lewis 2011

COUNTRYSIDE BOOKS
3 Catherine Road
Newbury, Berkshire

To view our complete range of books,
please visit us at
www.countrysidebooks.co.uk

ISBN 978 1 84674 267 5

Illustration on page 12 supplied by Simon Jardine, Armadillo Images

Designed by Peter Davies, Nautilus Design
Produced through MRM Associates Ltd., Reading
Printed by Information Press, Oxford

Contents

At times our underwear has been unhygienic, erotic, uncomfortable, ridiculous, painful, vulgar and funny.

Dulcie Lewis

The Corset, *an etching by J. Gillray, 1810.*

Casting Off the Corsets

GOING UNDERCOVER

Underwear will push, pull, lift, flatten and coerce less than perfect bodies into a more desirable shape – whatever fashion dictates. On the whole, the mechanics of underwear are hidden for, apart from naturists, most people remain covered. The British weather probably has a lot to do with it!

There are exceptions, however. On even the coldest Saturday night, the young woman out 'clubbing' remains resolutely uncovered – not a warm coat in sight. With a plunging neckline and a skirt barely hiding the pubic bone, underneath there is a brassiere, shaping a heaving breast, and a pair of strong pants curbing the rolls of fat.

Women in the past were not so brazen: society ladies and 'loose' women may have partly exposed their breasts in public, but legs remained covered. The underwear of respectable ladies stayed hidden, except for a hint of lace or *broderie anglaise,* but it was still there, heroically sculpting in all the right places.

At times our underwear made us ill. The image of the Victorian woman lying on her *chaise longue,* feeling unwell, was likely to be true – she could scarcely breathe, let alone take a brisk walk. In attempting to achieve an 'hour glass' figure, with the perfect 18-inch waist, she was lashed into a corset with the lacings pulled ever tighter by a strong maid. Internal organs were displaced and ribs moved, all so a Victorian gentleman could circle her waist with his hands. A man unlacing a woman from her corsets was a prelude to lovemaking; although given the length of time it took, some may well have lost the will to proceed.

TAKING THE AIR

Ma's out, Pa's out – let's talk rude:
Pee, po, belly, drawers.

Michael Flanders and Donald Swann, 1956

Once, women were without knickers. A little air between the legs was seen as healthy and no bad thing. There were a few

Two late Victorian chemises. One is plain but the other, with more broderie anglaise, *would have been for 'best'.*

A detail from a chemise. The flat covered buttons were made of brass so they could pass through the wringers of the mangle on washday.

exceptions, of course: the courtesans of Venice wore knickers in the early 1500s made of velvet or silk. The knicker was therefore synonymous with a louche lifestyle and no respectable woman considered wearing such a shameful undergarment.

A loose-fitting chemise, a couple of petticoats for warmth and a heavy skirt were enough to keep the draughts out and made a 'call of nature' relatively simple. Undergarments were rarely washed and outer garments made of such materials that washing would ruin them. The chemise next to the skin absorbed sweat and any other bodily secretions. Bathing was exceptional.

☙

Samuel Pepys kept his diary from 1660 to 1669, in which he recorded the smallest details of everyday life, and yet he only once mentioned his wife Elizabeth having a bath.

> *… my wife busy in going with her woman to the hot-house to bathe herself, after her long being within doors in the dirt, so that she now pretends to a resolution of being hereafter very clean. How long it will hold, I can guess. 21st February 1665.*

☙

Underwear makes me uncomfortable and besides my parts have to breathe.

Jean Harlow, 1911 –1937;
Hollywood film star known as the Blonde Bombshell.

☙

THE GREAT COVER UP

The simplicity and diaphanous fashions of the early 1800s needed an undergarment to cover women's private parts. Gone were the layers of petticoats and heavy skirts, instead low-cut and figure-hugging, empire-line dresses left little to the imagination and offered no warmth. In many cases young women literally did 'catch their death of cold'.

An etching from 1799 showing the revealing dresses of the period. The muffs carried in front were useful for preserving some modesty. (From Taste and Fashion, *1945.)*

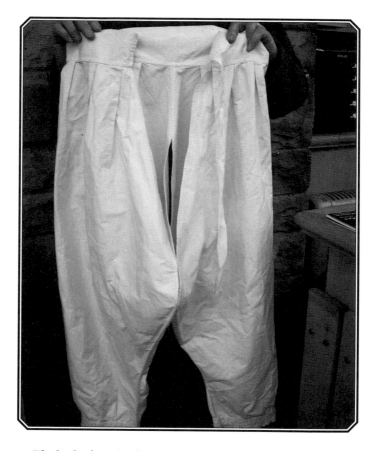

The back of a pair of Victorian divided, knee-length drawers, fastened at the waist by two long tapes or strings. (By kind permission of the Dales Countryside Museum, Hawes.)

The first knickers were known as pantaloons and reached down to below the knees. There was **no** gusset. The legs of the pantaloons were separate and attached to a band at the waist.

೧೦

Old Doctor: It's very cold today, Nellie – winter draws on.

Nellie: Aye, Doctor – I've just put them on.

೧೦

By the mid 1800s the Victorians had everyone in drawers. Made of white cotton or linen, knee- or ankle-length, with an edge of lace round the bottom of the leg and 'drawn up' around the waist. The divided drawers, still without a gusset, were essential as the Victorians had rejected Regency simplicity and returned to swathes of clothing worn over hooped and padded skirts.

It was a common theme among Victorian medical men that women had a bad habit of 'costiveness' – the tendency towards constipation. This can be understood, given the rigidity of the underwear. Answering a call of nature was not easy with the bottom half of the body inside a hoop and the top half held firmly in place with stays, corsets and boned bodices. The only way was to bend the knees and 'pee' through the gap in the drawers with all the clothes still in place. Thus, an upper class woman preserved her modesty.

೧೦

LÈSE-MAJESTÉ

Queen Victoria (1819–1901) always had a weight problem. As a young woman she ate too much, disliked taking exercise and often felt bilious. Her Majesty claimed to be 5 feet 3 inches in height but more reliable sources said 5 feet only. In 1838 at the age of 19, not yet married to Albert, she already weighed nearly 9 stone.

Queen Victoria's divided linen drawers dating from 1890. Remarkably plain and extremely large, they measure 36 ins/90 cm across. (Inset) Embroidered initials VR and crown on a linen chemise belonging to Queen Victoria. The chemise was number 4 of a batch of 12 or more. (By kind permission of David Clow.)

Casting Off the Corsets

The queen's drawers were of a generous size, and her monogram was embroidered onto them so there was no mistaking to whom they belonged!

Victoria preferred to wear her underwear for only a short time before donning new ones. The cast-off drawers were given away to members of her household at the royal palaces. The ones in the picture were given to a lady-in-waiting at Osborne House on the Isle of Wight. One of her descendants passed them to the owner of a drapery shop in Southsea in the late 1930s in payment of a debt. They are now in the possession of the drapery owner's grandson who, in 2010, took them along to the BBC's *Antiques Road Show* where they were valued at £300. A similar pair was recently sold at auction for the queenly sum of £3,000 – not a bad price for a pair of drawers.

༺༻

During the last years of her life, Victoria was said to have lost 3 inches in height. And after having given birth to nine children, her weight had probably doubled. It was not something she would have wished her subjects to discuss. Queen Victoria was always photographed sitting down, in a voluminous dress and shawl, often with relatives crowding round her, so it is hard to know. All things considered, her Majesty's underwear had to be of a generous size.

༺༻

A BLOOMING GOOD IDEA

Amelia Jenks Bloomer (1818–1894) was a fervent American campaigner on women's rights, temperance and dress reform. She edited the Ladies Temperance Society newspaper, *The Lily*, and campaigned for freedom from restrictive underwear and cumbersome clothes.

Bloomers were part of her healthy dress campaign. Her recommended outfit in 1851, for liberating young women, was a short jacket, full skirt to below the knees and bloomers, long loose 'Turkish-style' trousers, gathered at the ankles with a 2-inch ruffle. Mrs Bloomer was mocked but undaunted.

Bloomers were not popular with all women. Up to then women's legs had been hidden under skirts and hardly mentioned. The idea of wearing trousers, however loose, was too much and too masculine for many. Freedom of movement was fine but not at the cost of losing 'the male interest in our body'. American women were

Mrs Bloomer's outfit drew large crowds to her public lectures. The popularity of her Turkish trouser dress lasted only a short time. (From The Illustrated London News, *1851.)*

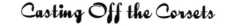

A Neat Figure, Real Comfort, and Delightful Freedom by wearing McCallum's Registered

Kals

Instead of Petticoats. Sample Pair, 3s. 11d., post free, in Navy Blue or Fawn. State size of Corset worn and your height.

If you wish, send to the Manageress for pattern of the material before ordering. Another pair GIVEN if they do not wear well for twelve months. Cycling Kals like these, 3s. 11d. and 5s. 11d.

Obtainable only from

KALS, Limited,
4, Stonehouse,
PLYMOUTH.

An alternative to petticoats. 'The soul of the modern woman hailed with delight the advent of cloth knickers and bloomers.' (*From* The Lady's World, 1898.)

liberated by bloomerism, British and European women less so. It was not until 1880 and the new craze for bicycling that Amelia's ideas on women's wear were accepted on both sides of the Atlantic.

OH, KNICKERS!

'Oh Knickers!' An exclamation of defiance or contempt.

∽

Correct underclothing, under all circumstances, shows a nicely balanced mind and a sense of the fitness of things, which some people can never acquire.

The Ethics of Underclothing, 1889

∽

It was not recommended that women should be without corsets altogether when cycling. A lighter, knitted corset gave support and 'protects the vital parts from chills'. (From The Lady's World, *1898.)*

A lady cyclist of the 1890s wearing the new knickerbockers,
plus tie, jacket, hat, gloves and gaiters.
(From Taste and Fashion, *1945.)*

Casting Off the Corsets

By the 1870s the gap had closed. Knickers referred to an undergarment with a gusset. It was an abbreviation of the word knickerbockers – short, baggy trousers gathered on a band at the knee and, until then, favoured by gentlemen for sporting casual dress. They were adopted by women under their dresses, but not everyone viewed them kindly.

༄

By 1890 knickerbockers were outer garments made of tweed and wool, worn by young women of the Rational Dress Society. They were determined to seize new opportunities and take part in activities previously open only to men. Such shocking pastimes as cycling, sport and mountaineering were now no longer precluded by weighty skirts.

༄

There was one corner of England, and a particular activity, that for many years still had a very practical use for a pair of knickers without a gusset – Kent hop pickers!

Hop Pickers' Knickers

There were no privies in the hop fields of Kent in the 1920s, judging by the antics of the women. They used a screen of picked hop hines when they were in need and they never pulled their skirts up. Most of them were in possession for hop picking of a type of knicker, 'two legs on tupe', as they called them. So you only had to squat and make out that you were picking up dropped hops.

From *Kent Privies* by Dulcie Lewis, 1996

HOW VULGAR !

RED HAT, NO KNICKERS

Red was the colour associated with royalty, revolution, the church and prostitution (the red light district). Women of easy virtue were thought to advertise their availability for sexual intercourse by wearing a red hat. The red hat may also have been a reference to the broad-brimmed, tasselled hat, the galero, known as The Red Hat, once worn by cardinals.

ALL FUR COAT AND NO KNICKERS

Before equal pay and women's liberation it was assumed that the only way a woman could afford a fur coat was through the generosity of a man, as a gift for her services.

TO GET ONE'S KNICKERS IN A TWIST

To be agitated and confused. A reference to a woman hurriedly getting dressed, perhaps after some scxual activity.

GET THE KNICKERS

In a British prison it once meant penal servitude, so-called because the convicts wore knickerbockers suits. The USA later adopted it as slang to mean 'a life sentence'.

A KICK IN THE PANTS

A setback, a hurtful remark or disappointment but has also taken on the meaning to urge someone on to greater effort.

EUPHEMISTICALLY SPEAKING

It is not surprising that such an intimate undergarment has a number of alternative names. These euphemisms most often refer to the size of our knickers, generous or otherwise, and to the protective qualities of being well covered:

Apple catchers

Bloomers – particularly large knickers.

Clouts – knickers or trousers (Yorkshire).

Drawers

Free traders – drawers with no gusset.

Knicks

Getting comfortable. Woollen and cotton underclothes 'For Ladies, Gentlemen & Children for all Climates'.
(From The Lady's World, *1898.)*

Pantaloon – named after Pantalone, a 16th-century Commedia dell'arte character. An elderly, unpleasant fellow who wore a tight-fitting red vest, breeches and stockings, and liked money and flirting with young girls.

Pantalettes – long drawers with lace round the bottom.

Stockinette combinations. (From The Lady's World, *1898.)*

Pants

Panties

Passion fuddlers

Passion killers

Smalls

Unmentionables

∽

In Northern Ireland, when a neighbour's washing line had a row of large knickers hanging out to dry, the comment made was, 'You've got a nice line of pocket handkerchiefs there.'

∽

Big bloomers hanging from the washing line in Bangor were called 'windsocks' – because you could see which way the wind was blowing.

∽

Aunt Hannah, a Blackpool boarding house landlady, said of large pants hanging on the washing line, 'You could fetch two stone of potatoes in those.'

∽

It is claimed that in some upmarket suburbs in America, drying clothes outside on a washing line is banned, as the size of some ladies' knickers causes distress.

A walker in the 1930s came across an isolated railway cottage

For warmer spring days, a combination garment of white calico, trimmed with lace. The pattern with instructions cost 6½d. (From The Lady's World, *1898.)*

in the Yorkshire Dales. Hanging on the washing line was a pair of large bloomers made of good quality cotton. Written in large letters across the back was **YORE MILL FLOUR.** The bloomers were home-made, using an old flour sack from the local flour mill at Aysgarth Falls.

FANCY PANTS

DIRECTOIRE: Long knickers gathered at the waist and round the leg, held in place with buttons or elastic. From the style favoured by upper class women during the French Directory period 1795 –1799.

TANGO KICKERS: Wide-legged to allow full movement when dancing the tango, a popular dance from 1914 onwards.

COMBINATIONS: Worn by both men and women for warmth. A long slit between the legs and at the back allowed ease of use when using the lavatory.

CAMIKNICKERS: A camisole – short bodice with knickers attached, often with a flap that buttoned between the legs. The shorter, slimmer fashions of the 1920s required less bulky underwear.

TEDDY: An American word for camiknickers.

FRENCH KNICKERS: Wide-legged knickers made from expensive material such as satin and silk, and very popular in the 1930s and 40s.

MAGIC KNICKERS: Many retailers now offer magic solutions to losing an inch in an instant and at the same time flattening tummies and lifting bottoms.

G-STRING/THONGS: Flimsy material just covering the female genitals and held in place between the buttocks and by elastic around the hips.

HOLDING IT TOGETHER

Rubberised yarn or elastic for keeping underwear on and up was generally available from the First World War (1914–1918) onwards. It was a welcome development after the intricate entanglements of tapes, buttons, hooks and eyes.

During the Second World War (1939–1945) the rubber plantations of Malaya were under the control of the Japanese and rubber for elastic was scarce. The weekly wash in boiling water took its toll on knicker elastic and a well-prepared woman always carried a safety pin.

༉

Aunt Dorothy went up to the farm and found Miss Bate fussing around prior to a visit to Wadebridge. She was getting in a panic, and asked Aunt Dorothy if she happened to have a safety pin, explaining, "I always put a safety pin in me drawers before I go to town, in case they fall down!"

From *Cornish Privies* by Sheila Bird, 2001

༉

A woman whilst in her privy way down her garden was heard to shout to her husband: "George, George, bring I a fork quick." George goes rushing down and hands her a garden fork.
"Not that sort of fork, you B…F…," she shouted. "I mean a fork what you eats yer dinner with. I got a knot on the 'lastic of me knickers, and until I gets it undone I can't sit down and have a good 'un."

From *Privies Galore* by Mollie Harris, 1990

༉

SHAPE SHIFTERS

Women have altered their shape throughout the centuries, whether it be adding to, or taking away. The breasts may be enlarged or reduced, the waist minimised, the hips and bottom padded or flattened and the stomach pulled in. The purpose of wearing such extravagant, even grotesque, structures as the farthingale, crinoline and the bustle in the past was to draw attention to the smallness of the waist. The skirt was a symbol of femininity, but what went on underneath so often served only to make life uncomfortable for the wearer.

THE FARTHINGALE: In Elizabethan times a skirt weighing 20 lbs had to be supported on a farthingale for the full effect. This large wooden or padded structure, worn in two parts, was attached to the waist and extended the hips sideways, giving the

'Alas Fido, we cannot pass and must retrace our steps.'

27

impression of giant panniers. It was a fashion worn by society ladies until the mid 1700s and a skirt width of 11 ft was not uncommon. Passing through narrow doorways was impossible, until the problem was solved by panniers made from whalebone that could be lowered by a piece of string. Some clergy believed that women kept men hidden under these enormous skirts.

៳

In the 17th century Oliver Cromwell brought a bill before Parliament against the '*Vice of painting and wearing Patches and immodest Dresses of Women*'. Included in this was legislation that if a woman trapped a man into marriage by presenting herself, not as nature intended, but with artificial teeth, iron stays, hoops or bolstered hips, she should be tried for witchcraft and the marriage annulled.

៳

THE CRINOLINE: A Victorian woman had a difficult life managing a magnificent skirt draped over a vast, bell-shaped cage, swelling towards the rear, and stuffed with quilted horsehair. Wearing this '*a lady may go through life without provoking the rude remarks of the observers*'. Alas, this modesty was easily compromised by a gust of wind or leaning too far in any one direction, as the skirt swung like the bell it resembled. The size of the skirt meant that it was virtually impossible for a Victorian gentleman to get anywhere near a Victorian lady when she was dressed.

THE BUSTLE: By the 1870s the crinoline was gone. A woman of fashion had a generous bosom, a tiny waist, all emphasised by a flattened, sweeping skirt at the front and a large framework

*Bustling along.
The height of fashion
from 1870.*

to support the fullness of the skirt behind. To achieve this S-shape still required a substantial wire cage. Sitting down was never easy.

❧

THE DONKEY AND THE BUSTLE

A young lady was walking sedately in the streets of Chester when a donkey began to follow her. She walked faster – trotted – then broke into a run. So did the donkey. And then, when she was fairly cornered, the donkey tore her skirts and underskirts away. The explanation? It lay in the trail of brown powder which marked the young lady's flight; her fashionable bustle was stuffed with bran!

From *Woman's Journal*, 1950

STAYS, CORSETS AND FAIRY BELTS

Happiness is the sublime moment when you get out of your corsets at night.

Attributed to Joyce Grenfell (1910–1979), humorist

∾

At first, women laced the bodice of a dress to give some shape and to pull in the waist. It is impossible to know the truth of a story that the first stays were invented by a 13th-century butcher to stop his wife from nagging. He laced her so tightly she could not draw enough breath to speak.

Stays were essentially early corsets strengthened with metal, wood and later, whalebone, sewn between layers of stiffened linen and fastened with lacings. A poor woman might have stays made of leather worn over a simple chemise and a skirt for her lower half. They were often her only possession of any value, to be pawned when times were hard. For the wealthy, stays remained out of sight, with additional stiffeners sewn into the dress.

Gradually, whalebone replaced iron. Whalebone became so popular that in 1722 the Low Countries borrowed heavily to promote whaling and meet the increasing demand for corsets stiffened with whalebone.

∾

The invention of the metal eyelet hole in 1828 strengthened the lacings even more. Waists got smaller.

∾

The emphasis was changing to one of comfort rather than 'compression' at all costs. (From The Lady's World, 1898.)

High-minded men were against corsets. Jean Jacques Rousseau (1712–1778), the great French philosopher, declared them to be *'the enemy of mankind'*.

Napoleon Bonaparte (1769–1821) Emperor of the French, strongly opposed the corset as, *'the implement of detestable coquetry which not only betrays a frivolous bent but forecasts the decline of humanity'*.

Medical doctors knew the damage done by tight corsets.

On the other hand, less principled men enjoyed the act of removing corsets from a lady.

∽

In Victorian England 'nice' girls wore corsets, 'bad' girls did not. Loose clothes meant loose morals. At puberty a girl's long hair was styled up and corsets went on.

Casting Off the Corsets

The Victorian Fairy Belt was designed specifically to achieve the longed for 'wasp waist'. Wearing this belt *'changes the form of the waist, making it look two to three inches smaller'*. The name gave the same hope that today's advanced technology designs hold – a shapely figure without effort.

∾

Sporting activities and corsets do not mix. The 1870s saw women playing a very sedate game of tennis on the lawns of country houses: it could not be otherwise with boned underwear and wearing a hat. Even when women became sufficiently emancipated to play championship tennis at Wimbledon in 1884, corsets were still worn and often blood-stained after a hard match. The magazine *Punch* remarked how difficult it was for women to play tennis in such tight underwear and that men should be similarly handicapped, by having a scarf tied round their knees.

The changing shape of corsets –1900 to 1904. The fashionable Edwardian woman favoured the full-bosomed, forward-thrusting, 'plump partridge' look.

A CHANGE OF UNDERWEAR

The First World War (1914–1918) changed everything. Women were needed to work for the war effort and replace the men away at the Front. For many women it was the first time they had earned their own money. Servants, including ladies' maids, were in short supply, so upper class women had fewer helpers to dress or fashion their elaborate hair styles. Drastic times called for radical measures, so out went the bustle, up went the skirt, off came the corset. The United States War Industries Board calculated that by giving up their corsets, American women had released 28,000 tons of steel for the war effort; enough for two battleships.

∽

Those men fortunate to return from the war were shocked to see the changes in their women. Not only had women cut their long hair but were seen powdering their noses in public, wearing lipstick and *learning to use the typewriter* – a previously male occupation.

Even some women thought it had all gone too far.

∽

How pleasant is the day when we give up striving to be young – or slender.
> William James (1842–1910), American psychologist.

∽

Petticoats – known as slips from 1920 onwards. Slimmer and shorter for the fashions of the 1920s.

Casting Off the Corsets

THE HON. LADY FORTESCUE IS APPALLED

What a much better chance we used to have of hiding our defects before the present fashions came into being! Now we must either expose our arms and legs to the critical and often unkind gaze of the world or be considered hopelessly old fashioned. No longer can the woman with 'bedpost legs' and 'gummy ankles' take refuge beneath a sheltering skirt or wear black stockings to minimise their proportions to the eye. She must emphasise their shape by donning nude coloured stockings and wear a skirt reaching only half-way down her legs – or even less far.

Modes and Morals, 1927

A FIRM FOUNDATION

At 50, you have the choice of keeping your face or your figure and it's much better to keep your face.

Barbara Cartland (1901–2000), author.

∽

Lady Fortescue declared that for the older woman '*modern fashions are nothing less than a tragedy*'. The whole emphasis had changed to making the female body more like that of a boy: slim-hipped, flat-bosomed, no curves, the waist no longer the focal point. Dieting and exercise were the order of the day. The Victorian and Edwardian ideal of an hourglass figure seemed hopelessly old-fashioned.

∽

Help was at hand for the woman with ample curves. The 1920s' full-length, heavy-duty corset with suspenders streamlined a body built on generous lines. Lacings were replaced by zips and a complete set of hooks and eyes, and the corset extended upwards to fully enclose the bust. Manufactured in rubber, the overall look was tightly controlled and with heavily-ribbed panels, made the wearer sweat, in spite of small air holes incorporated in some designs. The substantial seams marked the body temporarily with indentations and, on certain occasions, the corset was removed well beforehand, to allow the marks to disappear.

It was hay time and one of the married daughters went back to

Casting Off the Corsets

This corset emphasized the adjustable waist which '…trims and slims'. However, the sizing from 24 to 30 inches suggests that whoever bought this corset was already quite trim. (From Woman's Journal, *September 1950.)*

Kitten Hips **for you**

… in Sensation's little masterpiece 823!

Here's Sensation's famous adjustable waist. The waist that trims and slims. Sensation garments hold you, mould you —and don't forget they last deliciously!

823 comes in sizes 24″ → 30″

From all the better stores

Remember, if it's a belt, a bra, or a corselette it's wonderful to wear a

Sensation

KOPS BROS. (GT. BRITAIN) Ltd.
CAVENDISH HOUSE, 31-35 MORTIMER STREET, LONDON, W.1

A magnificent example of a corset – zip belt with downward stretch elastic, satin back, French elastic lace side panels, 6 suspenders, lightly-boned in front, designed and built for the medium to full figure. Price 60/-. But time is moving on…
(From Woman's Journal, *June 1953.)*

the family farm to help. Her job was on the hay mew, in the barn, trampling down the hay for winter storage. It was sweltering in the barn and the work was hot and dusty. That morning she had put on, without thinking, her rubber corsets with a full set of suspenders attached and the sweat was pouring from her. There was nothing for it but to take off her corsets and she hung them over one of the roof trusses but by the end of the day she had forgotten all about them. Fred the farmhand came across the corsets and was told to drop them off on his way home from work. Walking beside the railway track he met a linesman going about his duties. The linesman looked at the rolled up corset with the dangling suspenders under old Fred's arm, 'By heck Fred, what have you been up to?' In vain Fred protested that he had nothing to do with the removal of the lady's corsets but the linesman gave him an admiring grin and moved on up the line.

∾

Even for a young women with a good figure, the first corset was a rite of passage. The underwear section in any department store was discreetly at the back of the shop – just as it is today – away from prying male eyes. Judging from the number of newspaper advertisements, many women disliked shopping in public for such intimate garments and preferred buying their corsets through the post. Others had a saleswoman come to the house with a catalogue and samples. But change was coming. Apart from an older generation of women, quite happy with their well-built corsets, the days of the full-length corset were already numbered.

∾

The word 'corsetry' with all its connotations of restriction was replaced in 1922 by a new word 'lingerie'. From the French *linge* meaning 'linen'.

Casting Off the Corsets

THE YEARS ROLL ON

1930s New elasticised material could be manufactured as a tube. Hooks and eyes were obsolete; no longer a full-length corset, but a girdle, covering from the waist to the tops of the thighs. The girdle was rolled on and, with no seams or panels, gave a smoother line.

1940s Resources were concentrated on the war effort so women had to make do and mend. All clothing during the war had to adhere to Utility standards and bear the Utility logo due to shortages.

1950s New types of nylon and nylon blended with wool, cotton, satin and silk meant more flexible underwear. In 1954 the first corset was made from two-way stretch fabric.

1960s Lycra, a new synthetic yarn resembling elastic, was increasingly used for lingerie and swimwear. In 1961 Marks & Spencer introduced panty girdles to meet the growing trend for women to wear trousers.

༄

Brevity is the soul of lingerie.

Dorothy Parker (1893–1967), US writer.

༄

AN UPLIFTING EXPERIENCE

'*You don't get many of those to the pound*'– a vulgar expression used by the more coarse male, on seeing a young woman with large breasts.

ↄ☉

Men may admire a woman with an ample bosom but those who are well-endowed know that large, and with age, increasingly pendulous breasts are not all they are cracked up to be. In previous centuries, the big-breasted woman may have been fashionable and desirable but, for most of the time, she was just uncomfortable.

ↄ☉

Before the brassiere, women wore tight stays and stiffened outer bodices. The rigidity of the stays had the effect of pushing the breasts up and, depending on the impression you wished to make, it was up to the individual how much was exposed over the top of the chemise and bodice.

ↄ☉

In 17th-century France, ample ladies of the court used their bosoms to good effect. A deep and generous *décolletage* concealed a handkerchief, purse or even letters. Louis XIII used a pair of sugar tongs to retrieve a letter he wished to read from one such hiding place. A bosom bottle, a tin cone covered with ribbon, and lodged securely between the breasts, was a fashionable receptacle in which to arrange flowers tastefully across the chest. The wearing of such an ornament may have curtailed energetic dancing.

ↄ☉

Casting Off the Corsets

Apple dumpling shop – 18th-century slang for breasts.

∽

Marie Tucek patented her 'breast supporter' in America in 1893.

∽

Vogue magazine first used the word 'brassiere' in 1907.

∽

The idea of a separate support for the breasts had been around for a few years, especially with American women who wanted freedom of movement to pursue the sports and pastimes they saw men enjoying.

Mary Phelps-Jacob, an American socialite, fed up with her corset stays pushing up and showing above the neckline of her dress, is credited with inventing the modern brassiere. With the help of her maid, she devised a flimsy undergarment of two silk handkerchiefs tied together, baby ribbon sewn on for straps and a seam set in the front. It flattened rather than provided any uplift. She patented the idea in 1914.

∽

Bracière – an old French word for arm protection and referring to a military uniform. What we call a brassiere the French chose instead the name *soutien-gorge* – a throat support (throat was a euphemism for breast).

Other countries were more robust, using a word that translated into English as breast or bust holder.

Germany – *büstenhalter*
Denmark – *brystholdere*

Casting Off the Corsets

Brassiere and girdle very definitely separated by July 1955. (Courtesy of The M&S Company Archive.)

Holland – *bustehouder*
Sweden – *brösthållare or bysthållare*
Some English women never felt happy with the word *brassiere* – too foreign – and preferred *bust bodice*.

In 1926 Marks & Spencer started selling brassieres.

A Very Famous Brassiere

Jane Russell (1921–2011), the sultry Hollywood star, had a magnificent 38-inch bust. Howard Hughes, the aeronautics tycoon, was a huge admirer and said of her, 'There are two good reasons why men go to see her. Those are enough.' He directed her in *The Outlaw* but her quivering bust was too much for the Hollywood film censors of the day. Hughes designed 'the world's first cantilevered brassiere' for her but never realised the metal structure was too uncomfortable to wear. She quickly discarded it, returning to her old bra, but lining it with tissue to firm it up and stop the quivering.

∽

Bra Burning?

In 1968 women protesters at a Miss America beauty contest discussed burning uncomfortable underwear, including their bras but Health and Safety prevented it.

∽

FOR THE VERY LATEST

It is now possible to buy a brassiere for every occasion and in every possible configuration:

Backless • Bandeau • Front Fastening
Maternity • Minimiser • Multiway
Nursing • Push-ups • Sports • Strapless • T-shirt
And within those ranges there are:
Underwired • Non-wired • Padded • Non-padded
And there's even more choice, as all of the above come in a variety of shapes:
Plunge cup • Balcony cup • Full Cover cup • Demi cup
• and finally, ¾ cup

∽

Old age is when going without a bra pulls all the wrinkles out of your face.

Anon.

Spring 1968. Young women wanted less formal and rigid underwear. The brassiere was now known universally as the bra.
(Courtesy of The M&S Company Archive.)

43

SIZE DOES MATTER

It is claimed that the design of the wide-brimmed champagne glass was based on the shape of the breast of the French Queen, Marie Antoinette (1755–93).

∾

It soon became obvious that the early manufacture of brassieres in the three sizes of small, medium and large, failed to address the infinite variety of women's breasts. Research was conducted and by the 1920s the cup sizes A, B, C and D were universally acknowledged.

It was rumoured a number of years ago that the M.D. of an American underwear company never referred to A, B, C and D cups but instead to:

> Ping pong
> Ding dong
> King kong
> … and Holy cow!

∾

BOSOM FRIENDS

For women as flat as two poached eggs, there has always been subterfuge.

In the 1800s 'falsies' or 'gay deceivers' were made of wool placed inside the boned bodice.

The French wore rubber pads and called them 'lemon bosoms'.

In 1885 bust 'distenders' made of satin or Indian rubber were hidden inside a corset and inflated.

A 1900's advertisement for bust enhancers claimed, 'The fullness imparted is of lovely, perfectly natural proportions, impossible by unhealthy, always self proclaiming pads or breast forms. Our readers may test the genuineness of this unspeakable boon'.

From the 1950s onwards rubber and plastic inserts – or the cheap alternative of cotton wool – gave extra inches.

Modern-day bust enhancers are now easily obtained and are known, because of their close resemblance, as 'chicken fillets'.

∽

Brassiere cup sizes now range from A through to JJ. But the ultimate bust enhancer, increasingly used by today's celebrities, has to be surgical implants.

In the 1950s, brassieres became increasingly popular – a move away from the all-in-one corset and corselette. (From Woman's Journal, *May 1953.*)

MEN ONLY

A lot of men of a certain age have a furniture problem.

Their chest has fallen into their drawers.

∽

Men have worn underpants for centuries; made of woven or knitted linen, knee- or ankle-length, depending on the fashion of the time. When out riding, an additional undergarment of rabbit skin helped keep out the cold. Men's lower regions have always been covered up, warm and comfortable.

The only discomfort suffered by a man was the male corset, so essential for a man of fashion when style dictated an elegant figure. A slim waist was achieved by lacing and men consumed just as much whalebone in their corsets as women.

From the Prince Regent, later George IV (1762–1830), who became such a figure of ridicule, to Edward VII (1841–1910), kings, aristocrats and politicians have all crushed their mountainous flesh into male corsets.

∽

Briefly

BRIEFS – as the name suggests.

BUDGIE SMUGGLERS – coarse Australian slang for extremely brief swimming trunks.

BUM LIFT – underpants that lift a sagging bottom.

COMBINATIONS – an all-in-one top and bottom, favoured by men in the past to keep out the cold.

GIGILO PANTS – very brief underpants.

KECKS – underpants (West Riding of Yorkshire).

LININS – Geordie, as in, 'Hae ye got some clean linins for 's?' (Do you have any clean underpants for me?)

LONG JOHNS – woollen underpants down to the ankles. Rarely worn now except by Yorkshire farmers. Male golfers in the winter are known to wear their wives' tights, which have the same effect.

POSING POUCH – masculine equivalent of the G string and thong q.v.

Y-FRONTS – closely-fitting underpants with the front seams taking the form of an inverted Y

Knitted long johns from the 1940s, with a shorter version for summer.

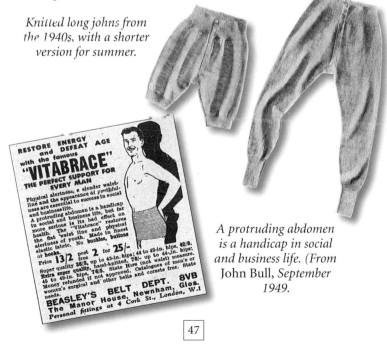

RESTORE ENERGY and DEFEAT AGE
with the famous
"VITABRACE"
THE PERFECT SUPPORT FOR EVERY MAN

Physical alertness, a slender waist-line and the appearance of youthful-ness are essential to success in social and business life.
A protruding abdomen is a handicap in social and business life, but far more serious in its bad effect on health. The "Vitabrace" restores the flat waist line and finest elastic fabric. Made in alertness of youth. No buckles, buttons or hooks.
Price **13/2** post **2 for 25/-**
free
Super quality 38/2, up to 43-in. hips; 44 to 49-in. hips, 42/9.
Extra super quality, 74/5, hand-knitted. 78/- up to 44-in. hips.
45 to 49-in. hips, 74/5. State Hips (not waist) measure.
Money refunded if not approved. Catalogues of men's or women's surgical and other belts and corsets free. State needs.
BEASLEY'S BELT DEPT. **8VB**
The Manor House, Newnham, Glos.
Personal fittings at 4 Cork St., London, W.1

A protruding abdomen is a handicap in social and business life. (From John Bull, September 1949.

THE LIBERTY BODICE

We owe much to American women when it comes to comfortable underwear. Initially, the liberty bodice was part of the American liberation movement before the First World War: getting women out of stays, corsets and bustles and into work and play. A liberty bodice offered some support, warmth … and liberty.

While women moved on to prettier lingerie, the young were stuck with the liberty bodice. It was the essential undergarment, not only for British schoolgirls, but also for young boys with a 'weak chest' who were humiliated by having to wear it. Before central heating, and when most children walked to school, it undoubtedly kept you warm but it was not loved. The liberty bodice was sleeveless and made of cotton, waist-length, fleecy-

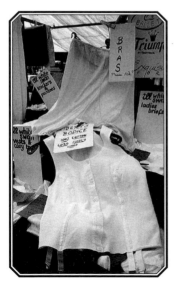

lined, with flat rubber buttons, fastening up the front and with extra buttons for attaching to knickers or suspenders.

At the first sign of puberty, girls wore thick lisle stockings held up by suspenders, buttoned to the liberty bodice. The suspenders were uncomfortable and ugly, and girls had various names for them – one being 'diddly-doddlers'.

An adult liberty bodice, including suspenders, on sale in a northern market town in the 1990s. Together with the bloomers, they are a very warm option.

THE BEST DAYS OF YOUR LIFE

Within living memory it was possible to arrive at school in the winter with the upper body layered in red flannel to keep the chest clear of coughs (brown paper, if you were poor), a woollen vest, liberty bodice, school blouse/shirt, cardigan/jumper and jacket. Poor children who were unlikely to bathe were once sewn into their vests in autumn and released in spring.

Regulation knickers were large, shapeless and built to last in thick botany yarn, with a generous gusset and worn with a liner which could be washed more often than the knickers. The elastic round the waistband and leg covered all flesh from the top of the leg to the waist. The small pocket on the side of the knicker leg, supposedly for a handkerchief, was used more often for stowing lumps of gristle from the school dinner. They were so substantial that after taking off the school skirt for P.E. and Games there was no need for further covering. At a Catholic boarding school in the 1960s, the nuns were concerned that regulation school knickers would excite lust. When the girls attended a school dance where boys from the neighbouring public school were going to be their dance partners, the nuns pinned the girls' knickers to their vests with safety pins.

Who's air-conditioned for comfort?

Aertex keeps children at a healthy even temperature right round the clock. In the heat of the day the special Aertex cellular weave ventilates and cools the body. But when the temperature drops it acts as an insulator, keeping out the cold and preventing chills.

There are Aertex shirts, underwear, pyjamas for men and boys; pyjamas, blouses, underwear for women and girls; corsets and babies wear, too! The coupon below will bring you full particulars.

Genuine Aertex bears this label

AERTEX

The bliss of Aertex after a woollen vest. (From Woman's Journal, *May 1953.)*

CARRY ON KNITTING

Lack of money and shortages of materials, both during and after the Second World War, together with an abhorrence of waste meant that women did their very best with limited resources. It was a time of 'make do and mend'. Mothers made dresses for their daughters from their own old clothes, with knickers to match, and short trousers for boys from father's trousers. Old knitted garments were unpicked and the wool reused. Underwear was darned and patched, while others went even further, knitting and crocheting a whole range of undergarments. Wearing wool, a natural fibre, next to the skin was thought healthy and so those who found woollen underwear made them itch were told there was a war on and not to complain.

CASTING ON

Knitted vests were easy and sometimes known as Spencers, after the 2nd Earl Spencer a 19th-century politician, who wore a short, waist-length jacket which was the original Spencer.

Knitted knickers did not last long unless they were lined.

Children's combinations of knitted vest and underpants, whilst warm in winter, proved too hot for summer.

Knitted or crocheted brassieres offered little support and were no good for large bosoms.

Knitted knee warmers were a comfort for the elderly.

Socks and stockings: *'To strengthen hand-knitted stockings, take a reel of strong thread and knit with the wool for the heels and toes. The wear is trebled and there is no sacrifice of comfort.'* (From *Home Hints*, 1930.)

Darning is a lost skill now but in hard times, even when well holed, a pair of socks was never thrown away. Men in the Armed Forces were good at darning and sailors knitted their own socks.

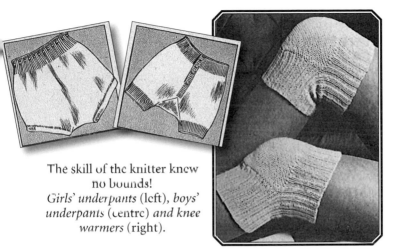

The skill of the knitter knew
no bounds!
Girls' underpants (left), *boys'
underpants* (centre) *and knee
warmers* (right).

Above all, hand-knitted underwear needed careful washing –
no Monday washday boiling.

୰୰

A knitted swimsuit is as useful as a chocolate teapot.

ဏၟ

The problems with a knitted bathing costume can be
understood immediately; even by those not forced to wear such
garments as children. Hugely popular during the 1930s, 40s, and
50s, they were fine for the beach, building sandcastles, paddling
and sunbathing but attempting to swim in them was another
matter. The wool took on water and the knitted costume sagged

alarmingly as it clung to the lower parts of the body, while leaving higher bits exposed. The swimmer was a sorry sight on emerging from the sea and drying the costume in the sun, while still wearing it, was an unpleasant business.

This did not stop the knitter, who once the children were kitted out, turned her knitting needles to the adult family members.

1930s' knitted bathing suits for adults. (Courtesy of Kathy Firth)

The shortages during the Second World War meant that knitted bathing suits for children were the only option. (Courtesy of Ray Lewis)

PETTICOAT RULES

If you cannot have a petticoat to match every costume, it is well to have a neat one of soft black silk, nicely cut and frilled. This cannot be offensive under any circumstances ... The great crime is to wear a petticoat which does not match or harmonise with the outer costume. In this matter French women are far and away ahead of us; they would never wear a costume of plum colour, and display on lifting it a scarlet petticoat.

From *The Ethics of Underclothing*, 1889.

For centuries, petticoats were a serious business: the front of a petticoat was designed to be seen. Richly decorated with gold and silver braid and a statement of wealth, many were of sufficient value to be gifted in a will.

Under the petticoats, tied either side of the waist, were two embroidered pockets on tape. An opening in the skirt allowed the wearer, or others, to reach into the pocket.

Lucy Locket lost her pocket,
Kitty Fisher found it;
Not a penny was there in it,
Only the ribbon round it.

Kitty Fisher was a great beauty at the court of George III, with a dubious reputation.

Casting Off the Corsets

A demure full-length slip from February 1955. (Courtesy of The M&S Company Archive.)

A pair of pockets from between 1725 and 1750 – crewel work on cotton. (By kind permission of the Swaledale Museum, Reeth, North Yorkshire.)

The early Victorians wore petticoats to excess. It was not uncommon for a lady of fashion to have seven petticoats, including one of red flannel for warmth, plus wads of horsehair for more width. The weight was considerable.

The cumbersome crinoline of the mid 1800s lasted for twenty

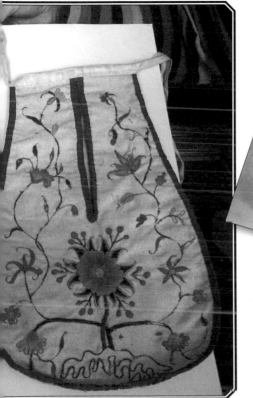

A long waist-length slip from October 1957. (Courtesy of The M&S Company Archive.)

years and for all its failings did give some respite from the layers of petticoats. The metal hoop provided the fullness and underneath, wearing the new drawers, legs were free. The crinoline went the way of all fashions and by the late 1800s petticoats had become simpler undergarments of beauty and therein lay temptation …

Casting Off the Corsets

The Ladies' World magazine of 1889 warned of: *A girl who coming to work in London, had resisted every temptation generally offered to a young woman alone in lodgings, until she accepted a silk petticoat from one of her male admirers. This was the beginning of her fall, she could not resist the glamour and the swish.*

ᏉᎧ

The new fashions of the 1920s required something sleeker: petticoats became known as 'slips' manufactured in chiffon, silk and crêpe de Chine, and all in lovely colours. Women revelled in their new freedoms, although not everyone had fun. It was grim for women school teachers:

You are not to keep company with men.
You may not loiter in ice-cream parlours.
You may not smoke cigarettes.
You may not dress in bright colours and you may not dye your hair.
You must wear at least 2 petticoats and your dresses must be no shorter than 2 inches above the ankle.

ᏉᎧ

For a short time in the late 1950s and early 1960s, multi layers of petticoats made a come-back, stiffened by a home-made solution of sugar and water. Young women danced in high-heeled 'winkle-picker' shoes and full skirts to Bill Haley and the Comets and a young Elvis. Rock and Roll and outrageous petticoats were part of teenage rebellion.

ᏉᎧ

SOMETHING SHOCKING

…he will come to her in yellow stockings, and 'tis a colour she abhors, and cross-gartered, a fashion she detests; and he will smile upon her…

From *Twelfth Night* by William Shakespeare.

The pompous and deluded steward Malvolio tricked into believing his mistress Olivia loves him.

∽

Woollen stockings have been worn for centuries. Finer-knitted stockings in linen thread, or silk for the very rich, were available in England from the mid 1500s. Female legs were not on show, but the wealthy Elizabethan man made much of his shapely calves in silk stockings, embroidered with clock motifs and other embellishments. The poor made do with plain wool and earned a living from knitting and crocheting stockings.

When an English clergyman invented a knitting frame, which would have put the knitters out of work, Elizabeth I refused his request for a patent, not wishing to cause unrest in the kingdom. The Reverend William Lee took himself and his machine off to France, where he was met with more enthusiasm.

But it was only a question of time and on his death the workers brought the machine back to Nottingham. By the early 1700s the new hosiery machines were well established.

∽

Stockings … made of wool, cotton thread, silk, beaver skin or cotton, knitted, woven or sewn, sometimes decorated with gold or silver clocks. In summertime females also wear them made of leather against gnat bites.

From *The Women's Encyclopaedia*, 1719.

'Water.' The Benefit of Crinoline, and Preservation of Life. *An 1859 lithograph showing a complete set of underwear: petticoats, the crinoline structure, drawers, white stockings and garters. (From* Taste and Fashion, *1945.)*

∾

White stockings were the most popular colour.

Violet stockings were worn by bishops.

Black stockings became fashionable towards the end of the 1800s.

Josephine, the first wife of Napoleon Bonaparte had 108 pairs of white stockings, and even more blue ones and 32 pairs in rose.

From 1912 stockings were produced in a neutral beige.

∽

A Blue Stocking – a nickname for a scholarly or intellectual woman. Originally a member of a society, formed in 1750, for high-class ladies who were well read and interested in new ideas. Wearing blue stockings marked them out as members.

∽

THE MOST NOBLE ORDER OF THE GARTER

Honi soit qui mal y pense
Evil be to him who thinks evil.

Or a more ribald version:
Honey sweet but smelly pants

It was Edward III's famous exclamation on catching sight of the Countess of Salisbury's garter. He went on to found the Order of the Garter, c.1347, the most senior order of British knighthood, whose distinguished members wear a dark blue velvet garter below the left knee, with the famous inscription in gold letters.

∽

No one likes a wrinkled stocking and a pair of garters did an adequate job of keeping the stockings up above the knee. However, there was more to the garter than the mere mechanics of holding up a stocking. It was imbued with a sexual charge more powerful than a simple circlet of knitted wool or velvet ribbons could possibly command. The garter nestled next to skin in secret places, only to be seen by a lover or husband.

It was the custom, at one time, for a man to wear a pretty girl's

The Second World War had just ended but there were still severe shortages. Stockings from a male admirer were an important gift. (From Illustrated Magazine, *October 1945.)*

garter in his hat or round his knee. At a wedding a bride wore a garter with ribbons which were distributed to the groom's friends. For a man, the garter was a trophy of sexual conquest; for a woman, a gift only she could bestow.

∽

The garters of society women and high-class courtesans were richly embroidered and encrusted with jewels. The Italian adventurer Casanova (1725–1798) wrote in his memoirs of one lover's garter, embroidered with words which had the effect when spoken aloud of 'inflaming both of us'.

∽

As stockings became longer and women more active, the garter was not enough. Edwardian corsets had suspenders with metal clasps. Suspenders took on the sexual connotations of the now redundant garter. For some men a suspender still has the same effect as the embellished garter so enjoyed by Casanova.

The 1920s 'flapper' shocked with her short hair, boyish figure and knee-length skirts. Silk stockings were on show.

In the 1930s, rayon made from cellulose fibre, replaced silk stockings.

1937 Du Pont of America announced a new material called nylon. Nylon stockings caused a sensation.

1939 to 1945 – the Second World War – rationing and shortages. With no silk or nylon stockings British women went barelegged and rubbed on gravy browning to give their legs colour; black eyeliner pencil created a faux seam at the back. This worked until it rained. American G.I.s in Britain were known to have nylons and, as with knicker elastic, a pair of nylons was a powerful male bargaining tool.

1960 The start of the Swinging Sixties and the mini skirt. Young women wanted fashions of their own, not just a version of what their mothers wore. Stockings and suspender belts were replaced by the comfort and freedom of a pair of tights. As

The Coronation of Queen Elizabeth II was held on 2nd June 1953 and a patriotic advertisement for stockings appeared. (From Woman's Journal, *June 1953.)*

A proud Tradition

The royal house of Tudor united the white rose of York and the red rose of Lancaster in the symbol of the Tudor rose—proudly used by the first Elizabeth.
So the 'Tudorose' mark to typify fine stockings in this Coronation year is fitting indeed.
Look for the Tudor rose with its double row of petals, on the 'Tudorose' box everywhere.

Tudorose *stockings*

NYLON * PURE SILK * LISLE * NYLON * PURE SILK * LISLE

women rejoiced, men were dismayed. The loss of the sexually-charged stockings and suspenders meant the last vestiges of uncomfortable underwear had been cast off.

Women were never to go back.

༺༻

In olden days a glimpse of stocking was looked on as something shocking, Now, heaven knows Anything goes!

From the 1930s' musical *Anything Goes* by Cole Porter.

Spring, 1968. Times were changing. Pretty panty girdles in plain and printed designs in Lycra, with detachable suspenders, were just part of the new freedoms enjoyed by those lucky enough to be young in the 1960s. (Courtesy of The M&S Company Archive.)

BIBLIOGRAPHY

Bardey, Catherine, *Lingerie – A History and Celebration of Silks, Satins, Laces, Linens and Other Bare Essentials*, 2001
Brewer's Dictionary of Phrase & Fable
Cassell's Dictionary of Slang
Deutch, Yvonne, *A Glimpse of Stocking – A Short History of Stockings*, 2002
Hawthorne, Rosemary, *Knickers – An Intimate Appraisal*, 1991
Laver, James, *Taste and Fashion*, 1945
Picard, Liza, *Restoration London*, 1997
Picard, Liza, *Dr Johnson's London*, 2001
Tabori, Paul, *The Art of Folly*, 1961
The Lady's World, 1898/99
Turner, Jean, *No Time Like The Past*, 1997

ACKNOWLEDGEMENTS

I only had to mention that I was writing a book about underwear and so many friends offered memories and thoughtful insights, not to mention their underwear, that it is difficult to list them all individually. However, grateful thanks must be given to the following:

Fellow members of Carperby Women's Institute and the TWITTS Walking Group.

Ann Holubecki for her, as always, generous contribution of memories, books and papers.

Elma Banks, Doreen Moore and Eleanor Scarr for the loan of underwear.

Casting Off the Corsets

My daughter Megan.

Kirsty Osborn.

I am also indebted to the following organisations:

The M&S Company Archive.

The Dales Countryside Museum at Hawes, North Yorkshire.

The Swaledale Museum at Reeth, North Yorkshire.

Liz Lawson at Wensleydale Press, Hawes, North Yorkshire.

And finally, my husband Ray, who could not offer much help on this subject, but could do all the cooking and cleaning while I was writing.